ORPHISM

ORPHISM

by

J. R. WATMOUGH

Late Senior Scholar of St Catharine's College, Cambridge;
Gladstone Student of St Deiniol's Library, Hawarden;
and Member of Gray's Inn.

CROMER GREEK PRIZE 1934

CAMBRIDGE

AT THE UNIVERSITY PRESS

1934

CAMBRIDGE
UNIVERSITY PRESS

University Printing House, Cambridge CB2 8BS, United Kingdom

Cambridge University Press is part of the University of Cambridge.

It furthers the University's mission by disseminating knowledge in the pursuit of education, learning and research at the highest international levels of excellence.

www.cambridge.org
Information on this title: www.cambridge.org/9781107497429

© Cambridge University Press 1934

This publication is in copyright. Subject to statutory exception and to the provisions of relevant collective licensing agreements, no reproduction of any part may take place without the written permission of Cambridge University Press.

First published 1934
First paperback edition 2015

A catalogue record for this publication is available from the British Library

ISBN 978-1-107-49742-9 Paperback

Cambridge University Press has no responsibility for the persistence or accuracy of URLs for external or third-party internet websites referred to in this publication, and does not guarantee that any content on such websites is, or will remain, accurate or appropriate.

CONTENTS

PREFACE

This short essay was written at St Deiniol's Library, Hawarden, during the summer of 1933. Its purpose is two-fold. First, I wish to demonstrate that the tradition of mysticism, reform, and subjective morality associated with the name of 'Orpheus' is no less characteristic of Greek thought than is the cult of the Olympian gods. Second, I wish to draw what seems to me the obvious analogy between ancient 'Orphism' and modern Protestantism. My debts of obligation are many. I must thank Professor F. M. Cornford and Dr W. H. S. Jones for first introducing me to the subject in their lectures. I must thank the Master of St Catharine's, Dr Rouse, Professor A. B. Cook, and Professor Hodson for reading my manuscript and making several valuable suggestions. I must thank Lord Gladstone of Hawarden and the Trustees of St Deiniol's Library for the hospitality and leisure necessary for authorship. Last, and by no means last, I must thank the Master and Fellows of St Catharine's College; who, together with the Syndics of the Press, have covered the entire costs of publication.

J. R. WATMOUGH

Cambridge
March 1934

PROLOGUE

THE SOURCES

THE SOURCES

NO LACK OF EVIDENCE

It is frequently said in histories of ancient thought that the evidence concerning 'Orphism' is very scanty, and that therefore no serious attempt can be made to appreciate its religious significance. This view, I maintain, is wrong. We have abundant material at our disposal, ranging in date from the sixth century B.C. to the fourth century A.D. The real difficulty is to *criticise* the sources; to draw a line of distinction between the reliable and the non-reliable. Why? Because the average Greek did not understand 'Orphism', any more than the unlettered Freemason or Roman Catholic to-day understands the historical origin of his religion, and the historical meaning of his ritual. The explanations that satisfy the ordinary man, in all ages and all civilisations, are not the true ones. Sometimes they are *vaticinia post eventum*; sometimes aetiological myths. To the unphilosophic Greek 'Orphism' probably meant nothing more than 'Initiation'. It would call up to the mind an image of secret societies, daubings with clay, ritual cleansings, abstinence from meat: to the philosopher on the other hand it would suggest a vague tendency or tradition of asceticism—

connected theoretically with the name of 'Orpheus', but hopelessly confused with other movements, other deities, other rites.

THE 'GREAT CLASSICAL WRITERS'

How far, for example, may we trust the authority of so-called 'Great classical writers'? How far may we trust Euripides, Plato, Aristophanes? Because among all the gods Eros and Dionysus alone are respected by Euripides, some have supposed that this tragedian was an 'Orphic'. Yet such a conclusion is not warranted by facts. It is no truer to call Euripides an 'Orphic' than to call Bernard Shaw a disciple of Bergson. Just as Shaw in *Man and Superman* was attracted by the doctrine of the *élan vital*, so Euripides in the *Bacchae* was inspired by the mystic enthusiasm of the Wine-god and his votaries. There was a certain element of poetry about their worship which appealed to the tragedian's sympathy. But he was never for one moment a convinced 'Orphic'; and in consequence the *Bacchae*, judged as a *whole*, cannot be counted as historical testimony. It is a fantasy of the imagination, in which 'Orpheus' and Dionysus cease to be human personalities and become mere symbols of an abstract passion in our nature. Euripides provides more valuable evidence in other plays, where a chance

4

utterance or an irrelevant remark puts us on the scent.[1]

Plato, though his philosophy is charged with the 'Orphic' spirit, is not to be accepted without question as an authority. 'Orphism' coloured his thought, moulded his genius, and caused his mind to think along certain lines; but we cannot deduce from his writings the doctrine of a historical 'Orpheus'. Plato was an 'Orphic' in the sense in which Dean Inge is a Neoplatonist. The mystic philosophy secretly inspired him, but it never supplanted his Platonism. It would be rash in the extreme to draw serious conclusions from the eschatological myths of the *Gorgias* and *Republic*. Like the *Timaeus* these are εἰκότες μῦθοι, mere images of the truth. Plato's real value as an authority lies in those passages here and there in the dialogues where he mentions 'Orpheus' and his followers incidentally.[2] Such testimonies are most reliable; for Plato—unlike Aristotle—tends to be scrupulously fair and scientific in the treatment of his predecessors.

As for Aristophanes, he is as trustworthy an authority on 'Orphism' as the *Doctor's Dilemma* is an authority on modern medicine. Like Lucian, he is a comedian and a satirist—one might almost

[1] E.g. *Hippolytus*, 952 *sq.*; fr. 475 (the *Cretans*), etc.
[2] E.g. *Cratylus*, 400c; *Rep.* 364b; *Laws*, 715e; *Gorgias*, 493a; *Phaedrus*, 250c; *Symp.* 179c; *Euthyd.* 277d; *Meno*, 81a (?).

say a *biassed* comedian and satirist; for he was very much a 'Man of Marathon', heartily sympathetic with the old régime and not a little suspicious of the new. Nevertheless there are several burlesques in Aristophanes which, when due discount has been allowed for poetic licence, provide much valuable evidence about the ceremonies of initiation.[1]

Of the other writers of the best period of Greek literature, Thucydides has practically no contribution to offer: Aeschylus is singularly devoid of useful evidence, though several inferences may be drawn from the prologue to the *Eumenides*:[2] Pindar in his epinician odes is Apolline, and therefore unlikely to yield much fruit; though there is a wonderful passage in the second Olympian, and the Dithyrambs and Dirges, though fragmentary, are pregnant with 'Orphic' influence;[3] Herodotus occasionally refers to 'Orphism', but his remarks show—as might be expected—that he had no clear conception in his own mind of who 'Orpheus' was, or how his followers differed from the Pythagoreans and Egyptians.[4]

[1] E.g. *Clouds*, 223 *sq.* with Dieterich's interpretation in *Rh. Mus.* 1893; *Frogs*, 324 *sq.*; *Birds*, 693–703.
[2] *Eum.* 1–30. Aristotle tells us that Aeschylus was initiated (*Ethics*, 1111a).
[3] *Olymp.* II, 55–80; cf. also VI, 95–6; *Pyth.* IV, 176–7.
[4] Herod. II, 51, 81, 122.

Sophocles, religious though he was, has little to say on this subject.[1] He was a champion of the traditional state religion—very reverent, very uncritical, very respectable. Hence it is unlikely from the start that he would understand, or receive with sympathy, a creed so essentially new and non-conformist. We might with equal profit turn to the discourses of an educated country squire in the nineteenth century for scientific evidence of the rise of Congregationalism.

Mention should certainly be made of Pythagoras and Philolaus, who absorbed 'Orphism' into the religious side of their own tradition, though they left no reliable testimonies at first hand; of Cratinus the comic poet; of Empedocles, whose *Purifications* are thought by some to reflect 'Orphic' influence;[2] and of Heraclitus, whose later fragments deserve attention.[3] Empedocles is still a problem of dispute, and much depends on what interpretation we adopt. There is demonstrable proof that he believed in the fall of the soul and transmigration, but neither of these tenets is peculiar to the religion of 'Orpheus'. Heraclitus too is very puzzling. The ancients called him ὁ σκοτεινός. Let us accept their wise decision, and refrain from using him as positive testimony; for at best his criticism is adverse and

[1] See especially fr. 724, 753 (Nauck).
[2] Esp. fr. 115, 117 (Diels).   [3] Fr. 27, 124–30 (Diels).

7

prejudiced. The *Way of Opinion* of Parmenides is also dangerous ground.[1]

Our earliest authorities are probably the interpolations of Onomacritus (?) in the *Odyssey*; certain of the Homeric or so-called Homeric hymns; and certain passages in Hesiod.[2] If these could be proved to contain genuine 'Orphic' teaching, their value would be greatly enhanced. As it is they are vague. Scholars assume that they are 'Orphic' because they resemble the 'Orphism' of which we read in the Platonic Myths and other similar sources. 'Orpheus', Dionysus, Demeter, Persephone, Triptolemus, are all jumbled together in hopeless and inextricable confusion. We find an apocalyptic scene in Homer which appears to be inconsistent with the Homeric religion, or evidence of some sacramental rite in a later hymn—and conclude that, because 'Orphism' appears to have presented some teaching about the future life, and because the initiates in its mysteries held a sort of Eucharist, these passages are 'Orphic'. I do not suggest that this inference is necessarily wrong. I merely wish to interpose a word of warning against conclusions that are not strictly scientific.

[1] Burnet sees in this an affinity to the Myth of Er, which is usually accepted as Orphico-Pythagorean.

[2] E.g. *Od.* xi, 565–627; *Iliad*, vi, 132 (?); *Hymn to Demeter*, 206–11, 473–90; *Hymn to Ares*; Hesiod, *Works*, 737–41; *Theogony*, 411.

LATER AUTHORITIES

Later authorities are very numerous. It appears at first an almost impossible task to appraise their relative merits. In the fourth century B.C. we have a fragmentary dialogue Τηλαυγής by Aeschines of Sphettus, which represents Socrates as ridiculing an extreme form of asceticism. There is the speech of Andocides *De Mysteriis*—partisan evidence, as might be expected in a law-court speech. Demosthenes in the *Crown* rebukes Aeschines for participating in some mystery religion which may or may not be 'Orphic'. Aristotle has occasional remarks which mostly confirm what we already knew from other sources. Later still we have the *Characters* of Theophrastus —especially the 'Superstitious Man';[1] the sixth book of Virgil's *Aeneid*; much valuable evidence in Ovid's *Fasti*, if we may apply with wisdom and skill the method of 'inverse deduction' from the present to the past; much that is useful in Plutarch's *Moralia*.[2] Plutarch was a conservative, and a supporter of the traditional faith; but in his attempted justifications of this he gives the clue to many details of ritual. He tends, however, to be better at asking questions than at answering the same.

[1] With Jebb's notes.
[2] Esp. *De superstitione, De Iside et Osiride, De sollertia animalium, De esu carnium.*

9

There are the Lives of Diogenes Laertius, especially the Life of Pythagoras, the very naïveté of which testifies to a certain nucleus of genuineness; also scattered notices in Strabo, Suidas, Eustathius, Harpocration, Psellus and Proclus. Nonnus' *Dionysiaca* is useful; as also is the collection of 'Orphic' hymns[1]. There is the priceless guide-book of Pausanias; there are Porphyry's four books *On abstinence from animal flesh*, which throw considerable light on all the ancient ascetic movements; finally there are the Christian Fathers,[2] whose evidence is very copious, but very unreliable, since they wrote with obvious bias against pagan religions, and frequently reveal the coarseness of their own minds by interpreting in an evil light mystic ceremonies which we know from other authorities to have been merely symbolic. Any stick was good enough to beat an 'Orphic' with.

MOST VALUABLE SOURCES

After thus reviewing the whole range of ancient literature, it may be asked "Where then is the most reliable authority to be found?" The answer is: "In the apparently trivial remains of antiquity; in the power which modern archae-

---

[1] Ed. Abel (Leipzig, 1885); O. Kern (1922).

[2] Esp. Clem. Alex. *Exhortation to the Greeks* and pseudo-Hippolytus, *Philosophoumena*.

ology and comparative religion have given us of drawing inferences from other cults, and reconstructing the past from survivals in later generations". The incidents of ritual preserved, often unconsciously, on vase paintings are of supreme importance.[1] The scholiasts' notes on writers like Aristophanes and Euripides, if accepted with criticism, can be very valuable;[2] as can also the inscriptions on tombstones.[3] Etymology often gives a clue when other evidence is wanting. Above all, we have the aetiological myths by which civilisation attempts to justify savagery; and by which tradition preserved the relics of bygone days in all their crudeness and simplicity. These are at times more reliable in leading us to the truth than either satirists like Lucian and Aristophanes, or sublime philosophers like Plato and Pythagoras. The unconscious witness is always safer than the conscious.

[1] E.g. the fact that 'Orpheus' rarely appears on black-figured vases proves his lateness; whereas a literary reference like the παλαιὸς λόγος in Plato's *Laws*, 715e (said by the scholiast to be 'Orphic') might lead us to assume that he was early.

[2] For facts of course, not interpretations.

[3] Esp. the eight 'Orphic' tablets (ed. G. Murray in Jane Harrison's *Prolegomena*).

PART ONE

THE 'ORPHEUS' OF HISTORY

ἔφυγον κακόν, εὗρον ἄμεινον

THE 'ORPHEUS' OF HISTORY

GENERAL CONFUSION OF THE SUBJECT

Of all movements in Greek religious thought, 'Orphism'—the so-called tradition of 'Orpheus' —is perhaps the most confused: partly because of the halo of legend which has centred round its founder; partly because of its intricate entanglement with other cults or schools of philosophic speculation. On the religious side it has become associated with the worship of Dionysus in Thrace and Demeter at Eleusis: on the philosophic with Pythagorean mathematics and Platonic metaphysics. That the Greeks were no wiser than ourselves in this matter is shown by the well-known statement of Herodotus in Book II.[1] Orphic, Bacchic, Pythagorean and Egyptian almost meant the same.

The pursuit of an original, historical 'Orpheus' has been attempted with widely different results by various critics. Maass,[2] taking his stand on etymology, derived the name 'Orpheus' from ὀρφνή (darkness) and argued from this a chthonic deity—perhaps the counterpart of Dionysus in

[1] Herod. II, 81: ὁμολογέουσι δὲ ταῦτα τοῖσι Ὀρφικοῖσι καλευμένοισι καὶ Βακχικοῖσι, ἐοῦσι δὲ Αἰγυπτίοισι καὶ Πυθαγορείοισι.

[2] E. W. Maass, *Orpheus* (1895).

the underworld. Miss Harrison,[1] elaborating her thesis that all the bright and human in Greek religion was a late development superimposed on earlier bogey worship and apotropaic ritual, saw in the gentle lyre player and sun watcher a prophet whose mission was to spiritualise and sublimate the barbarism of Bacchic revelry. Reinach[2] saw in 'Orpheus' a fox totem of the Bassarids. Most scholars, on the grounds of lack of evidence, refuse to commit themselves to any definite opinion. Many would regard 'Orpheus' in the religious sphere as they regard Lycurgus in the political—a semi-mythical figure, to whom all changes and reforms are attributed.

THE 'ORPHIC' PHENOMENON COMMON TO MANY RELIGIONS

To debate whether 'Orpheus' was or was not a historical figure is in some ways wasted energy.[3] With our present evidence, abundant though it is, a scientific investigator is bound to remain

[1] J. E. Harrison, *Prolegomena* (1903), Chs. 9–12 with appendix.

[2] S. Reinach, *Cultes, Mythes et Religions* (1906) and articles in *Rev. Arch.* 1899 and 1900.

[3] The chief contributions to this subject, other than those already mentioned, are: O. Gruppe, article in Roscher (vol. 3); O. Kern, *Orpheus* (1920). See too the works of Lobeck, Farnell, Cook, Nilsson, Jevons, Rose, and Macchioro.

agnostic; and in any case the really significant truth lies in another direction—in the fact that an 'Orphic' movement seems to have occurred in many other religions than the Greek. Scholars, seeing this, have tried to argue that 'Orphism' 'came from Egypt', 'came from India', 'came from Thrace', 'came from Crete'; on the grounds of a similarity to certain religious beliefs and customs prevalent in those countries. This view is not impossible, but it is hard to acquiesce in. Religion is a conservative force and tends to spread slowly. When we reflect how long it took Christianity to become established in the Roman Empire—that too in the early centuries A.D. when travel was easy and political organisation convenient; it seems incredible that in the almost prehistoric centuries B.C. a cult of religious reform and mysticism should have been communicated from a single source over so wide an area as Thrace in the north, Crete and Egypt in the south, and India in the extreme east.

The explanation that an 'Orphic' movement is a spontaneous and indigenous growth in the evolution of almost every religion seems to be more attractive. I do not say that this is demonstrable: it merely *seems* on *a priori* grounds a probability. It does not, of course, rule out the possibility of an historical person 'Orpheus'. Just as in political history there is usually a move from kingship to oligarchy and oligarchy to democracy (not from oligarchy to kingship and kingship to democracy); so in religion the natural transition is from a ceremonial worship imposed by civil or ecclesiastical authority to a more spiritual and inward relation of the individual soul with God. That such a phenomenon is common to many nations, and due to more or less universal causes, is to my mind proved by the fourth book of Porphyry's *De Abstinentia*.[1] The devout and peace-loving Neoplatonist enumerates the various tribes and sects which in the past had abstained from animal flesh—the Egyptian priesthood, the Brahmins and Samanaeans in India, the Essene Jews, the Cretan priests of Zeus, and so forth. On analysis it is found that these have more characteristics in common than mere vegetarianism. They all have mystic communions and ritual purifications; all wear the symbolic white raiment and devote themselves to prayer and self-examination; they have a deep sense of personal sin and the accompanying hope of immortality; most of them are separate from, often indifferent to, their state religion; they are eager above everything to 'Become like God' (ὁμοίωσις τῷ θεῷ). In some cases there is a belief in the transmigration of souls; sometimes also a rule of abstinence from marriage and other forms of sexual

[1] Ed. A. Nauck (Leipzig, 1886).

intercourse. In a word they are, one and all, 'Orphics'.

FOUR POSSIBLE EXPLANATIONS OF THIS

If it is unlikely that any connection should have been established between these peoples, what generic causes can be assigned to their parallel development? Here we enter at once into the realm of speculation. A fertile imagination could invent many reasons. The late Prof. Bury[1] suggested that economic considerations might have been in part responsible. Poverty, due to over-population or lack of natural wealth, drives men to the supernatural. As long as they thrive in plenty, their religion, like that of the Homeric Achaeans, is a sanguine and optimistic enjoyment: but when 'the land is full of ills, of ills the sea', a sense of imperfection is begotten. God comes to the fore; the need of prayer and holy living is felt. A second explanation may be the inadequacy of traditional state religion to satisfy the growing inclination to mysticism. The man of mystic temperament, who has discovered the divine in his own heart, who seeks nourishment from above in deep, ecstatic revelations, is bound to recoil—if not in disgust, at least in indifference —from the purely political ceremonies of ortho-doxy. Third, there is the inevitable searching of

[1] *Hist. of Greece*, p. 313.

the human mind for moral sanctions. Hitherto
'good' and 'bad' have been mere aspects of social
order—that which is νόμῳ and that which is not
νόμῳ. The absurdity of such a criterion becomes
more and more patent as the human being becomes more heavenward in his aspirations; until
finally he founds a new religion which will satisfy
his conscience better. Fourth and last, there is
that sudden burst of light which comes at a
certain stage in the mind's development, bringing
with it an irrepressible impulse to *reform*.

It is on the note of reform that I would lay most
emphasis here. The sixth century B.C. has been
called on many grounds the Greek Renaissance.
The term is not strictly applicable, inasmuch as
there was only Birth and not Re-birth; but that
is a trivial issue. The sixth century saw the first
attempt at drama; the first serious attempt in
Athens to make a city beautiful for its own sake;
above all it saw the origins of Ionian science, the
first awakening of the mind to wonder how and
why. Was it merely accidental that this century
saw the advent of 'Orphism' in its fullest glory?[1]
I suggest that it was the natural result of a natural
cause.

[1] There were of course *suggestions* of 'Orphism' in the
seventh century, just as there were *suggestions* of the Protestant Reformation long before the traditional age of
Renaissance. Cf. the Homeric hymns to Ares and Demeter;
also parts of Hesiod (*Works*, 737 *sq.*, *Theogony*, 411).

'ORPHISM' PRE-EMINENTLY A RELIGION
OF REFORM, LIKE MODERN
PROTESTANTISM

That ancient 'Orphism', like modern Protestantism, *was* a religion of reform, seems clear from
more than one source of evidence. Strabo, a late
though on the whole reliable authority, writing
in the seventh book of his geography,[1] happens
to mention the village of Pimpleia at the foot
of Olympus. Here, he says, was the home of
'Orpheus'; a prophet, a seer, a juggler (γόης—
the same word which Euripides uses of Dionysus
in the *Bacchae*),[2] who at first busied himself with
lyre-playing, divination, and orgiastic rites, but
later became more aggressive (μειζόνων ἀξιοῦντα
ἑαυτόν) and tried to convert the multitude. Some
were willing proselytes: others regarded him—
like all reformers—with suspicion; for they feared
he was plotting against them, trying to under-
mine their established convictions, scheming to
destroy the *status quo*. So they made away with

---

[1] Strabo, VII, 18: ἐνταῦθα τὸν Ὀρφέα διατρῖψαί φασι τὸν
Κίκονα, ἄνδρα γόητα ἀπὸ μουσικῆς ἅμα καὶ μαντικῆς καὶ τῶν
περὶ τὰς τελετὰς ὀργιασμῶν ἀγυρτεύοντα τὸ πρῶτον, εἶτ' ἤδη
καὶ μειζόνων ἀξιοῦντα ἑαυτὸν καὶ ὄχλον καὶ δύναμιν κατασκευαζό-
μενον· τοὺς μὲν οὖν ἑκουσίως ἀποδέχεσθαι, τινὰς δὲ ὑπιδομένους
ἐπιβουλὴν καὶ βίαν ἐπισυστάντας διαφθεῖραι αὐτόν.

[2] Eur. *Bacchae*, 234: γόης ἐπῳδός.

him (διαφθεῖραι αὐτόν), and he died a martyr's death—the price of all reform in this conservative world.

Diodorus, if we may believe his statements, confirms this view; actually telling us the object of 'Orpheus'' reform, namely the rites of Dionysus. 'Orpheus' was not a god but a man, excelling beyond all other men in natural gifts and culture. He was a descendant of the god Dionysus, through the mediation of his father Oiagreus; and effected so many changes in the traditional rites he inherited that they lost their title 'Dionysiac' and became 'Orphic'.[1] Much in this account is probably mythical; and if Diodorus were the only authority, his statement would be discounted. But when supported by other testimonies, it seems fair to credit it with a germ of truth.

When a dignitary, civil or ecclesiastical, is excessively angry with a newcomer, the chances are a thousand to one that the newcomer is trying to criticise, supplant or reform the established régime. This is the conclusion suggested by Philostratus, when in his Life of Apollonius of Tyana[2] he quotes the words of Apollo, the Delphic god,

[1] Diodorus, III, 64: πολλὰ μεταθεῖναι τῶν ἐν τοῖς ὀργίοις, διὸ καὶ τὰς ὑπὸ τοῦ Διονύσου γενομένας τελετάς, Ὀρφικὰς προσαγορευθῆναι.

[2] IV, 14: πέπαυσο, ἔφη, τῶν ἐμῶν, καὶ γὰρ δὴ καὶ ᾀδοντά σε ἱκανῶς ἤνεγκα.

to 'Orpheus', who apparently had been issuing
oracles on his own account. "Hands off my
privileges! I have tolerated you enough—you
and your prophesying!"[1] The question may be
asked: why does 'Orpheus' here supplant Apollo,
and not Dionysus, as in the previous testimony of
Diodorus? Was he a reformer of Apolline as well
as Dionysiac religion? No certain answer can be
vouchsafed. Possibly he was an opponent of
traditionalism in *all* its forms, so that Delphic no
less than Dionysiac would come beneath his ban.
Possibly Apollo was Sun-god as well as god of
Delphi; and 'Orpheus' we know was interested
in the sun, for a vase painting in the Berlin
Museum[2] represents him as gazing upward into
the heavens; while the 'Orphic' parody in Aristophanes' *Clouds* reveals Socrates contemplating the
same celestial power.[3] However, this issue is irrelevant: the important fact is the fact that
'Orpheus' stands for *reform*.

Further evidence can be deduced from the
martyrdom by Thracian women. That such
martyrdom did take place is guaranteed not only
by the unanimous testimony of tradition in all
parts of the Greek world, but also by the archaeo-

[1] This scene is depicted on vase paintings.
[2] Catalogue no. 3172.
[3] *Clouds*, 225: ἀεροβατῶ καὶ περιφρονῶ τὸν ἥλιον. That this
is 'Orphic' has been proved by Dieterich (*Rh. Mus.* 1893).
See also the same writer's *Nekuia* (1913).

logical evidence of a hero shrine.[1] When the question of interpretation arises, many solutions can be offered. Did 'Orpheus' hate women, having lost his own wife Eurydice? Was he being punished, like Prometheus, for revealing the mysteries of Zeus? Possibly he died a death like that of the god he served—a literal σπαραγμός. Possibly he was a teacher of ascetic views which infuriated the other sex. But most likely, as Aeschylus seems to have thought,[2] he was martyred by Maenads, representative of the old traditional cult of Dionysus—the object of his contempt. Aeschylus as a religious critic was far in advance of his age, and his judgment therefore is most trustworthy.

At any rate the combined evidence of Strabo, Diodorus, Philostratus and Aeschylus furnishes demonstrable proof that 'Orpheus'—whoever he may have been, and whenever he may have lived —was concerned with the business of *reform*. Reform is begotten of reason, not emotion. So

---

[1] Conon xLv tells us that this was closed to women: ἔστι δὲ γυναιξὶ παντελῶς ἄβατον. This is hard to reconcile with our knowledge from other sources that the 'Orphics' —at any rate the Pythagorean 'Orphics'—exalted the position of women. Clement of Alexandria (*Strom.* IV, 19) for instance mentions a woman as editor of certain Bacchic writings concerning the mysteries. Cratinus ridicules the "Pythagorean women".

[2] Aesch. fr. 23–5. (With the comment of Eratosthenes, Καταστερισμοί, 24, 140.)

24

with 'Orpheus'. He was no rationalist philosopher; but when he looked around and saw the wild, barbaric, savage rites of Dionysus degrading their votaries into brutal superstition, he felt most earnestly the need for calming influences, the sober medicine of ὁσιότης and ἀποχή.

If we investigate the nature of reform and the peculiar excellence of reformers, we find that as a rule they provoke much irritation and unrest. Often they end in persecution and martyrdom. Why? Because there is in our human nature a certain element of pride and self-congratulation which engenders the spirit of conservatism. We have a strong and deep-rooted dislike of criticism, especially criticism from our social inferiors. For a 'Reformer' to talk about 'Improvement' gives inexcusable offence, because it assumes a present state of imperfection which might conceivably be made better. On the other hand reformers are sometimes genuinely reprehensible. There is a certain temperament which thinks of itself as inherently superior to its neighbours; which in its conceit pretends to divine illumination, and occupies its time on earth in establishing its own conception of heaven. As the Volstead act has shown, it is not long before the exiles for conscience's sake become the persecutors.

SOME LESS KNOWN ASPECTS OF 'ORPHISM' COMPARED TO SIMILAR TRAITS IN PROTESTANTISM

(a) *Its priggishness.* On its darker and less noble side, this strain of anti-social priggishness is seen in 'Orphism'. It is a characteristic which has not been much developed in the past, but I stress it here because it seems to me an essential element in all reform—especially in the Protestant reform of Christianity, whose parallelism with the 'Orphic' movement I am particularly concerned to establish. Let us examine the testimonies. Pausanias[1] in describing the musical contests at Delphi relates the following myth. There was one very ancient contest in which competitors must sing a hymn to the gods. Prizes had been won by Chrysothemis, Philammon and Thamyris, but 'Orpheus' and his son Musaeus refused to compete—such was their arrogance concerning their own rites (σεμνολογίᾳ τῇ ἐπὶ τελεταῖς), and their self-esteem in general (ὑπὸ φρονήματος τοῦ ἄλλου). Turn now to Aristophanes. In the parody of 'Orphic' ceremonial in the *Clouds*,[2] Strepsiades, about to be initiated, asks what he stands to gain thereby. "Oh", says Socrates, "you will become most skilled at vaunting, showing off, and being

[1] Pausanias, x, 7, 2: Ὀρφέα δὲ...ἐξετάʒεσθαι.
[2] *Clouds*, 260: λέγειν γενήσει τρῖμμα, κρόταλον, παιπάλη.

clever." Literally "you will become at talking like the fine flour that is ground from barley". Turn again to Euripides.[1] Theseus is taunting Hippolytus for his asceticism, his abstinence from flesh food. "Go, take 'Orpheus' for your king, for you are caught. I warn all men to shun you. Your like hunt souls, with proud, high-sounding words; scheming evil all the time." Demosthenes rebukes the 'Orphic' Aeschines[2] for his smug hypocrisy—because he pretends to be superior, and has found a better way than his companions. Adam has shown in his edition of the *Republic* that whenever Plato wishes to refer allusively to the 'Orphics' he calls them σοφοί (clever, pretentious)—the very word which Euripides uses of Dionysus in the *Bacchae*:[3] "Clever dog! clever dog! clever in everything but cleverness." Even in the old maxim "Many are the thyrsus-bearers, but few are the Bacchanals"[4] can be traced a note of priggishness. The real, spiritual worshippers of Dionysus—the 'Orphics' as opposed

---

[1] Eur. *Hipp.* 955:
τοὺς δὲ τοιούτους ἐγώ
φεύγειν προφωνῶ πᾶσι· θηρεύουσι γὰρ
σεμνοῖς λόγοισιν, αἰσχρὰ μηχανώμενοι.

[2] Dem. *Crown*, 259: κελεύων λέγειν 'Ἔφυγον κακόν, εὗρον ἄμεινον', ἐπὶ τῷ μηδένα πώποτε τηλικοῦτ' ὀλολύξαι σεμνυνόμενοι.

[3] Eur. *Bacchae*, 655: σοφός, σοφὸς σύ, πλὴν ἃ δεῖ σ' εἶναι σοφόν. Cf. Adam, *Republic* II, 378 *sq.*

[4] Apud Plato, *Phaedo*, 69c: πολλοὶ μὲν ναρθηκοφόροι, παῦροι δέ τε Βάκχοι.

to the mere ritualists who carry thyrsi—are few in number. They are an exclusive, superior set.

I do not suggest that entrance to their society was in any way restricted. So far as our evidence is trustworthy, any citizen of any status could be initiated. When I say the 'Orphics' were superior and exclusive, I apply the terms in the sense in which they could be used of Protestantism in Victorian England or Renaissance Geneva. There is in both these religious movements, if we examine their darker side, an element of self-righteousness, perhaps even hypocrisy, which the Greek tried to express by the words σεμνός and σεμνύνομαι. The ancient 'Orphic' would on no account touch meat or sacrifice an animal: adulteresses were excluded permanently from the Mysteries.[1] The Protestant to-day is frequently a supporter of Sabbatarianism and total abstinence: yesterday he ostracised illegitimate children from society. 'Orphic' and Protestant may both be right, and history is possibly on their side. With that I am not concerned. The important inference is this—in taking such a view, they irritate and annoy their neighbours. They are regarded by their more secular contemporaries as anti-social.

(b) *Its dissenting nature.* Such a charge in the case of the 'Orphics' was aggravated by the dis-

[1] Cf. Farnell, *Higher Aspects of Greek Religion*, pp. 38, 41.

sentient nature of their religion in general. 'Orphism' was essentially non-conformist. It was the first attempt in the history of Greek thought to break away from established traditions and 'political' theology. Religious dissent, as a result of the peculiar developments of Christianity in the nineteenth century, has acquired a significance which perhaps obscures the real issue. Dissent in my meaning applies not to the apostasy of individuals from a religious institution, but the secession of *all* the religious from *all* the secular. The 'Orphics' were, amongt he Greeks, the first dissenters in this respect. There was not the slightest suggestion of religious *persecution*, except in one case which we shall presently discuss. Indeed the whole theory of inquisitions and heresies was foreign to the spirit of the Greeks; such blasphemy trials as did take place being, like those of Anaxagoras and Socrates, entirely political in origin.[1] Inquisitions and heresies are only possible in degraded civilisations, where the mind is fettered and theological accuracy is made the criterion of salvation. The watchword of the Greeks was always ἐλευθερία.

The 'Orphics' therefore were not heretics. They were merely dissenters in the sense that they broke away completely from the cult of the

[1] This point is proved by J. B. Bury, *History of Freedom of Thought*, ch. 1.

Olympic pantheon. The established state-religion, based on the legends of Homer and Hesiod, was in their opinion not only immoral, in that it compelled its votaries to slay innocent animals, but destitute of all spiritual meaning. It was a commercial transaction between god and man. The notions of *moral* sin, *moral* purification, and *moral* holiness were never for one moment suggested. The idea of an immortal soul, if it existed at all, was interpreted only in the light of superstitious bogey-worship.[1]

The tendence of the Olympic gods was entirely the business of the city-state as a public institution. It involved the performance of various sacrifices, at various seasons of the year, according to the particular deity concerned. Outward conformity with these rites was expected much in the same way as nowadays outward respect is required towards prayers for the King's Majesty. The 'Orphics' broke away—not in the sense that they became actively hostile, but in the sense of realising that this was not religion. Religion was a relation between the individual soul and God, an escaping from this world's things to the things of eternity,[2] for the achieving of which end the necessary communal organisa-

---

[1] See Rohde, *Psyche*, passim; also Leaf's appendix on *Iliad*, XXIII.

[2] Cf. the Compagno tablet, θεὸς δ' ἔσῃ ἀντὶ βροτοῖο.

tion was not the state, but a brotherhood of an
entirely religious nature. If we turn to Porphyry[1]
we find that all the ancient ascetic movements
worked through this channel. The Brahmins had
their monastic houses in the secluded mountain
ranges of India; the Essene Jews had societies of
their own in every city—and so forth. The
'Orphics' called their communities θίασοι;[2] and
these were as different from the πόλις on the
religious, as ἑταιρεῖαι were on the political side.

How far these θίασοι were dissentient bodies can
be inferred from the especially interesting, though
perhaps exceptional, case of Croton in South
Italy. This city was the domicile of the Pythagorean order—not a pure 'Orphic' sect, because
the worship was concerned with Apollo instead
of Dionysus,[3] but similar in most essentials. It
was a sort of 'Rule of the Saints'. Starting as an
independent body, it soon found that the only
way of attaining recognition and authority was
to identify itself with the πόλις. Like the Calvinists at Geneva, therefore, the Pythagoreans
secured the sovereign power. Their reign was
intolerable, and a revolution followed in which
the civil dominion was restored (c. 450 B.C.).

[1] *De abstinentia*, IV, passim. For the Brahmins see 17–18;
the Essenes 11–14.
[2] Supposed to be derived from the root ΘΕΣ "to pray"
(θεός, etc.).
[3] Burnet, *Early Greek Philosophy*, p. 98.

Brief though it was, this attempt at theocracy is very illuminating. The first essential is to decide how far its downfall was an instance of religious persecution. Burnet answers in the affirmative: "We can still imagine and sympathise with the irritation felt by the plain man of those days at having his legislation done for him by a set of incomprehensible pedants, who made a point of abstaining from beans, and would not let him beat his own dog because they recognised in its howls the voice of a departed friend".[1] If this view is correct, the incidents at Croton are the only example of a genuinely religious persecution in Greek history. Even then the provoking cause was not dissent so much as tyranny. Kylon and his supporters cared not one jot or one tittle what the Pythagoreans believed: their fury was only aroused when the Pythagoreans began to enforce their beliefs on others. Mark the analogy with certain forms of Protestantism. It is the inherent nature of all dissent, when it has gained political power, to change its attitude and become the persecutor.

(c) *Its popular misrepresentations.* Criticism of 'Orphism' as a movement of reform is not complete unless some slight notice is taken of certain popular misrepresentations which, in the opinion of many scholars, approximate to quackery. If

[1] Burnet, *op. cit.*

we consider reform in the abstract we find that it
appeals as an idea to some sections of a community more than others—this too for different
reasons. It appeals to the high philosophic minds
like Plato and Euripides, Mill and Bentham, because of its own inherent worth; because it leads
mankind a stage nearer to the truth; because it
lifts them out of darkness into light. It appeals to
the middle classes, because they are the prudish,
respectable section of society—and, as we have
already shown, there is always an element of
prudery and respectability about reform. Lastly,
it appeals to the very ignorant and very superstitious, by reason of its fantastic idealism. Poor,
silly people are captivated by the nonsense which
reformers talk about a golden age to come; they
grasp eagerly at the idea of some miraculous
intervention, which will charm away their mis-
fortunes and bring a glimpse of heaven to earth.
In certain of the many ramifications of Modern
Protestantism this last phenomenon is all too
common. It is equally common, indeed, in
Catholicism; but the idea of the supernatural and
the priestly is there more prominent than the
notion of reform. Protestantism, feeling the hand
of authority less firmly, has greater scope for
imaginative development, and wider oppor-
tunities for pandering to superstition. There are
the Millenarians, the British Israelites, and count-

less others one could mention, whose appeal is popular and whose following is confined either to the ignoramus or to the fanatic.

Let us examine their parallel among the ancient 'Orphics'. Among the treatises ascribed to Hippocrates is a discourse on the *Sacred Disease*. This disease, he says, was due to no known cause; and the men who first attributed to it a sacred character were religionists of professed piety and superior knowledge.[1] As a remedy they prescribed purifications, and abstinence from certain foods—an 'Orphic' life in fact. By their sayings and devices they pretended to greater enlightenment, and deceived men by their talk of cleansings and lustrations, and by their much discourse about God and the Spirit.[2] 'Hippocrates' knows better. The disease, he claims, is entirely natural; and the miraculous cures are not miracles at all, but impostures.

Turn now to the second book of Plato's *Republic*.[3] *A propos* of a discussion of justice and

[1] *Sacred Disease*, 2: μάγοι τε καὶ καθάρται καὶ ἀγύρται καὶ ἀλαζόνες, οὗτοι δὲ καὶ προσποιέονται σφόδρα θεοσέβεες εἶναι καὶ πλέον τι εἰδέναι.

[2] *Ibid.* 10: τοιαῦτα λέγοντες καὶ μηχανώμενοι προσποιέονται πλέον τι εἰδέναι, καὶ ἀνθρώπους ἐξαπατῶσι προστιθέμενοι αὐτοῖς ἁγνείας τε καὶ καθαρσίας, ὅ τε πολὺς αὐτοῖς τοῦ λόγου ἐς τὸ θεῖον ἀφῆκει καὶ τὸ δαιμόνιον.

[3] *Republic*, II, 364 b: ἀγύρται δὲ καὶ μάντεις ἐπὶ πλουσίων θύρας ἰόντες πείθουσιν ὡς ἔστι παρὰ σφίσι δύναμις ἐκ θεῶν πορι-

the apparent inequality of the just man's lot, Adimantus quotes the case of itinerant 'Orphics' who go round to rich men's doors offering salvation, freedom from all sorrow and injustice, a life of pleasure and festivity, by means of enchantments and persuasion of the gods. These quacks win over, says Adimantus, not only individuals but whole cities, and their teaching even extends to theories of the future life by which the wicked can be bought off from their punishments. Here the parallel is more akin to the Roman doctrine of purgatory,[1] though there are Protestant Fundamentalists who believe most vehemently in Hell fires, from which only the 'saved' can escape.

Two more quotations, one from Demosthenes and one from Theophrastus, testify to the same spirit, the same outlook, in later generations.

In the *Crown* oration, Demosthenes ridicules Aeschines for his association with religious brotherhoods (θίασοι) which practise initiatory and purificatory ceremonies. Although the name of 'Orpheus' is not mentioned specifically, there

---

ζομένη θυσίαις τε καὶ ἐπῳδαῖς, εἴτε τι ἀδίκημά του γέγονεν αὐτοῦ ἢ προγόνων, ἀκεῖσθαι μεθ' ἡδονῶν τε καὶ ἑορτῶν. *Ibid.* 364e: πείθοντες οὐ μόνον ἰδιώτας ἀλλὰ καὶ πόλεις, ὡς ἄρα λύσεις τε καὶ καθαρμοὶ ἀδικημάτων διὰ θυσιῶν καὶ παιδιᾶς ἡδονῶν εἰσὶ μὲν ἔτι ζῶσιν, εἰσὶ δὲ καὶ τελευτήσασιν, ἃς δὴ τελετὰς καλοῦσιν, ἃς τῶν ἐκεῖ κακῶν ἀπολύουσιν ἡμᾶς, μὴ θύσαντας δὲ δεινὰ περιμένει.

[1] Some have compared Tetzel's sale of Indulgences.

seems little doubt that these brotherhoods taught
a popularised and degraded 'Orphism'. We have
already noted the similarity between their maxim
"Evil have I fled; better have I found" and the
Protestant reformers' doctrine of being 'saved'.
Let us further compare their behaviour in the
streets with that of the Salvation Army. These
men, says Demosthenes,[1] in the day-time lead
their processions through the public thorough-
fares, crowned with garlands of fennel and white
poplar, hugging serpents and shrieking out their
ancient counterpart of "Glory Hallelujah". The
old women welcome them with mystic names—
'Ivy-bearer' (κιττοφόρος), 'Basket-bearer' (λικ-
νοφόρος)—no doubt the equivalent of Major
Barbara and her companions. As their fees, they
receive loaves of bread and new-baked cakes.

We pass without further comment to Theophrastus, who in his picture of the superstitious
man refers to similar tendencies, reflecting pre-
sumably true characteristics of Greek society in
his time.[2] There is, he says, a certain type of man
who will approach neither a tomb nor anything

---

[1] *De Corona*, 260: θιάσους ἄγων διὰ τῶν ὁδῶν...καὶ βοῶν
'εὐοῖ σαβοῖ'.

[2] Theophrastus, XVI, 9: οὔτε ἐπιβῆναι μνήματι οὔτ' ἐπὶ
νεκρὸν οὔτ' ἐπὶ λεχὼ ἐλθεῖν...τελεσθησόμενος πρὸς τοὺς 'Ορφεοτε-
λεστὰς κατὰ μῆνα πορεύεσθαι. The avoidance of death and
childbirth among the Cretan mystics (whom Jane Harrison
believes to be 'Orphic') is testified by Porphyry, *De
Abst.* IV, 19.

associated with death or childbirth. This same man is initiated into 'Orphic' ceremonies, and visits the ministrants every month for preparation. His wife goes with him; or, if his wife has no leisure (here is a humorous sidelight on the attitude of women to 'Orphism'), he takes his children and their nurse.

Would it be a caricature to suggest parallels in Protestant Christianity?—remembering that we are concerned with the multitude, not the philosophic few. There is among certain Protestants the inherent feeling that it is 'not respectable' to discuss and criticise the dead. "De mortuis nil nisi bonum." There is also a superstition that all references to maternity, and the natural methods of generation therein involved, are improper. The subject is kept secret; it is treated as taboo; the language used to describe it is always euphemistic. The Catholic attitude on the other hand is different. The poor Irish Catholics in Liverpool view their departed friends as so many living souls gone to purgatory, to be released from the same by prayers and masses. The Protestant feeling of respectability and taboo is completely absent. Likewise in matters of marriage and sex, the uneducated Catholic, though his Church in theory exacts a very high standard of morality, in practice feels little sense of restraint, and rarely uses the euphemistic language of the Protestant.

The Catholic is in relation to the Protestant what the religion of Dionysus was to 'Orphism'.

GENERAL CRITIQUE OF THE MOVEMENT IN HISTORY

'Orphism' was a religion of reform. To sum up we can do no better than quote the words of Cornford:[1] "Orphism stands for a religious revival, one of those reformations which come, not by the rational contrivance of a political or ecclesiastical hierarchy, but by a spontaneous uprush from the perennial sources of religious feeling in the unconscious mind of a people. In such a case, when the official forms of religion have ceased to satisfy spiritual needs, the wind of the spirit may trouble to their depths the waters that had sunk to stillness. Out of these depths arise once more primeval images of thought and modes of feeling, which the rational mind had learnt to despise, as the grotesque and incredible play of mythical fantasy. Abandoned forms of ritual symbolism are resuscitated and invested with what presents itself as newly revealed significance. In this way the religious consciousness, bursting its too narrow confines, seems at once to soar upward and to plunge downward; and the onlooker is puzzled, and perhaps repelled, by the strange spectacle of a cult both more spiritual and less civilized than any within the range of established observance".

[1] *Camb. Anc. Hist.* IV, 533.

PART TWO

THE 'ORPHEUS' OF RELIGION

ἁγνείη δ' ἐστὶ φρονεῖν ὅσια

THE 'ORPHEUS' OF RELIGION

TRADITIONAL GREEK RELIGION
COMPARED WITH THE
MEDIAEVAL CHURCH

The mediaeval Church was in a sense profoundly religious, but only in theory monotheistic. More responsive to the authority of one Body than the concept of one God, it paid its sincerest devotions to the numerous aspects of the Blessed Virgin and the Saints. It received within itself the essentials of many strange religions, both literally and metaphorically pagan, surrounding with the halo of Christianity much that was fundamentally alien to Christ. To search for God in sacred writings, by the guidance only of the human reason, was as blasphemous in the attempt as it was damnable in the accomplishment. Neither was the witness of the Middle Ages in matters of morality *positively* virtuous. Its conscience was better pleased with the performance of ritual acts, with the riddance of evil spirits by fasting and confession, with *negative* means of grace, than with the genuinely spontaneous impulse of the soul in search of Deity.

Very similar was the state of Greek religion before the advent of 'Orphism'. Heaven was

populated with a noisy family of immoral, sensuous and stupid dummies; as devoid of godlike
as they were full of human characteristics; the
mere projections of man's own imagination. The
divine was not one, but many. Even a comparative late-comer like Dionysus is not Dionysus
alone, but Bromios, Braites, Sabazios, Zagreus,
Nyktelios, Omestes and Isodaites. In each aspect
he has his own peculiar ritual, his own peculiar
worship, like Our Lady of the Roses, Our Lady
of Lourdes, Our Lady Star of the Sea. To
'Become like God' or to approximate in any way
to the attributes of the divine was deadly sin.
"The brazen heaven man may not climb", says
Pindar.[1] That would be ὕβρις.

WHAT 'ORPHISM' INTRODUCED

(I) MONOTHEISM

'Orpheus' came, like the Protestant reformers,
to give new meaning to old superstitions; to purge
religion of all that was of the senses and degrading; to teach man to become himself a god—
in this world if possible, otherwise in the next.
He saw the futility, the ridiculous inconsistency,
of a polytheistic faith; aspiring rather (I say
'aspiring' because the ideal was not, and could

---

[1] Pythian, x, 27: ὁ χάλκεος οὐρανὸς οὔ ποτ' ἀμβατὸς αὐτῷ.

not have been, accomplished) after a vague and spiritualised monotheism. Like Euripides, the so-called 'Orpheus' knew that the "Father and Son were one God".[1] He saw too that holiness, the living of a moral life, the being like God, meant a subjective state of the worshipper; not the supernatural and miraculous gift of some external power. Compare this with Luther's maxim that "the just shall live by faith alone".

Monotheism and subjective morality are not ends to be achieved instantaneously. The many do not, all of a sudden, combine themselves into the one. The phenomenal does not become by revolution the real. So it is with little surprise that we find 'Orphism' retaining, sometimes consciously, sometimes unconsciously, traces of the old religion which to the superficial observer seem repugnant, superstitious and barbarian—wild-bull feasts, ceremonial purifications, scrupulous rules of initiation, indeed all the 'paraphernalia' of ancient ritual and mythology. The 'Orphic' was sufficiently enlightened to see that these alone were not enough; that over and beyond all human institutions was the great ideal of ὁμοίωσις, "Be ye perfect, as your Father in heaven is perfect"; but he had not the moral courage, he had not the necessary detachment from inherited mental environment, to break

[1] Clem. Alex. *Strom.* v, 688.

away completely from tradition, describing his new religion as it were on a clean slate.

Exactly the same can be said of the Protestant Reformation. Luther, Cranmer, Ridley, Latimer —all the champions of reformed religion in that era—were born and bred in an atmosphere of tradition. They inherited certain preconceived methods of thought and principles of behaviour. The world around them accepted the sacerdotal theory of the Church, the Mass, the Apostolic succession, priestly absolution and so on, as the natural order of things. To break away completely was, in the imperfect state of human nature, impossible. Man is in spite of himself a gregarious animal. He is tied down to the standards and criteria of his fellows; and however strongly he feels the impulse to ascend into realms of light, he is always partly fettered by the chains of darkness. Luther was convinced above all that only faith can justify; yet his altar still retained the inscription *Hoc est corpus meum*, implying, as we know from other sources, the whole Catholic theory of priestly mediation. The present authorised prayer book of the Anglican Church (1662) in spirit everywhere reveals a straining after individualised, subjective—what is popularly known as Protestant—religion; yet it still grants a place of high honour to the virginity of Mary, and in practice tolerates her invocation, together with the Saints, as a mediator; it still retains a prayer of absolution at Mattins and Evensong, and in the Communion of the Sick, which is meaningless unless we presuppose supernatural powers bestowed by Apostolic succession. It also retains in its Eucharist prayers from the Roman Missal which flatly contradict the spirit of its own rubrics.

This was the fate of 'Orphism'. Such literature as we possess, especially in later times, reveals most marked aspirations after a monotheistic conception of the divine; yet in practice it preserved to the end the *dramatis personae* of the old religion of Dionysus, which it superseded and reformed. In those mystery rites such as the ἱερὸς γάμος, though spiritualised in theory, the old symbols of licence and sex worship were still retained. Human nature, in the 'Orphic' no less than in ourselves, is conservative; and no matter how firm the conviction that change is necessary, vestiges of the old régime are slow to be obliterated. On the other hand, that the 'Orphic' movement did from the start achieve *some* contribution to the religion of liberalism and the spirit is demonstrable from the absence both of a logically formulated theology and a rigidly circumscribed priesthood.

45

(2) A SENSE OF SIN AND EVIL
IN THE INDIVIDUAL

If monotheism was the ideal of 'Orpheus' in the region of the divine and metaphysical, a sense of sin and evil was his greatest discovery as regards the individual and human. This theory deserves discussion at some length, because of its affinity to the more 'Evangelical' developments of modern Protestantism.

Personal sin was, generally speaking, a factor unknown in the pre-Homeric and Homeric ages. A sense of distinction between good and evil was not lacking; indeed, among the heroes of the *Iliad* and *Odyssey* there was a strong sense of honour and chivalry. "Hateful unto me as the gates of Hades is the man that sayeth one thing with his lips, but hideth another in his heart", says Achilles; implying a fairly high standard of personal and social morality, but not necessarily a sense of sin. By 'sin' is meant not merely error, nor indeed crime; but that deep sense of the imperfection of all human things which inspired the psalm *De profundis*. The human heart becomes aware of its own utter worthlessness, its inherent and essential vanity, its loneliness, its isolation from the Wholly Other. A feeling of sin of this kind was as foreign to the Homeric hero as to the religion he served. It was equally foreign to the pre-Homeric age of sprites and bogeys, where evil was not a moral force but an object of superstitious fear. The advent of sin synchronised with the advent of the first great personal religion—'Orphism'.

Corollaries of this:

α. *Transmigration of souls.* Of the corollaries of sin, the first that strikes the mind is transmigration. Wherever we find the 'Orphic' phenomenon, we invariably find an established belief in the pre-existence of the human soul, and its transmigration to some other human or animal being after death. The mere belief in transmigration alone is nothing new, and nothing peculiar to 'Orphism'. On the contrary it is very ancient. Plato calls it a παλαιὸς λόγος.[1] If we may guess at its origin, a plausible suggestion would be that primitive man, puzzled about the fact of the origin of life and unable to account for the creation of a new, except from an old, soul, invented transmigration as a sort of aetiological myth. The real significance of 'Orphism' is that it transformed this primitive idea into a means of moral and spiritual purification. When Empe-

---

[1] *Phaedo,* 70 c: παλαιὸς μὲν οὖν ἐστι τις λόγος, οὗ μεμνήμεθα κ.τ.λ.

docles said that "he had e'er now been a bush, a
bird, and a scaly fish in the sea",[1] he meant that
he had all but completed the penance due to sin.
His soul at the beginning of its existence had been
imprisoned in a mortal body. Why? Because it
was alien to God. On and on it had travelled
through the whole range of fleshly creation,
expiating the guilt by degrees, and striving to
become more akin to the divine. At the end of
its wearisome journey it would cast its earthly
tabernacle aside with joy, and become "an immortal god, no longer mortal".[2] That under
'Orphic' influences this old doctrine of transmigration ceased to be a mere explanation of the
perpetuity of animate life and became charged
with the deepest religious significance, offering
release from sin and evil, is abundantly clear
from the golden tablets found in lower Italy. "I
have escaped from the sorrowful weary wheel",
"I have paid the penalty for deeds unright-
eous".[3]

β. *The ascetic life.* The second corollary of

[1] Fr. 117 (Diels):
   ἤδη γάρ ποτ' ἐγὼ γενόμην κοῦρός τε κόρη τε
   θάμνος τ' οἰωνός τε καὶ ἔξαλος ἔλλοπος ἰχθύς.

[2] Fr. 112 (Diels):
   χαίρετ', ἐγὼ δ' ὕμμιν θεὸς ἄμβροτος, οὐκέτι θνητός.

[3] Campagno tablet (no. 5):
   —κύκλου δ' ἐξέπταν βαρυπένθεος ἀργαλέοιο
   —ποινὰν δ' ἀνταπέτεισ' ἔργων ἕνεκ' οὐχὶ δικαίων.

personal sin is the ascetic life. Whenever a human being is convinced that the origin of evil lies in matter, he is faced with two alternative methods of escape—either he must so far intoxicate the body that the soul is set free by the ecstasy of drunkenness, or he must discipline his flesh and keep its impulses in subjection. Dionysus chose the former, 'Orpheus' the latter method. Like transmigration, the ascetic ideal was nothing new; but it can claim under 'Orphic' influence to have acquired a new significance, just as the discipline of the monasteries acquired a new significance with the Protestant reformation. The pre-Homeric religion of aversion (ἀποτροπή) had its ascetic side in ceremonial fasts and purifications. Our sources for this stage of religion are indeed scanty,[1] but by means of the Aristotelian method of inverse deduction we can infer from the ritual of the sixth and fifth centuries B.C. the preliminary fasts which preceded the eating of sacred things in centuries long before. Take an example. We know that in historical times the second day of the Thesmophoria was a fast (νηστεία).[2] There is also demonstrable evidence from etymology and ritual that the Thesmophoria

[1] One of the most reliable testimonies is that of Plato, *Laws*, 782 c: ἀλλ' Ὀρφικοί τινες λεγόμενοι βίοι ἐγίγνοντο ἡμῶν τοῖς τότε.

[2] Athenaeus, 307f: Θεσμοφορίων τὴν μέσην, ὅτι δίκην κεστρέων νηστεύομεν.

was a later, and Olympianised, form of a much more primitive and apotropaic festival.[1] We therefore conclude that the fasting likewise was in main essentials primaeval. Ceremonial fastings may possibly have been associated with taboo and nature worship—an imitation, for instance, of the poverty of the earth in winter. The important fact is that they were devoid of moral and spiritual significance. With 'Orphism' much of the ritualistic and ceremonial element is retained, but behind there is much more real and much more personal yearning to escape from an abstract power called Evil. The physical, anthropomorphic conception of evil sprites and bogeys is still partially retained as the inevitable channel in which the thought of that time must be expressed;[2] but now and then we catch a glimpse of the real spirit of 'Orphic' asceticism, as in the beautiful fragment of Empedocles 'Fast from Evil'.[3]

The parallel in modern Protestantism is clear to the most superficial observer. Mediaeval monasticism, taking its stand on the later Apostolic and Patristic custom, imposed a ceremonial fast from meat and, according to some authorities,

---

[1] This is proved by J. E. Harrison, *Prolegomena*, ch. 4.

[2] In the ritual at Eleusis for example, where ceremonial fasting was still prescribed. Cf. Clem. Alex. *Exhortation*, II, 18: ἔστι τὸ σύνθημα Ἐλευσινίων Ἐνήστευσα κ.τ.λ.

[3] Fr. 144 (Diels): νηστεῦσαι κακότητος.

from sexual intercourse[1] on all recipients of the sacrament. It also preserved very rigorously the literal meaning of Lent. The sixteenth century reformers, who compiled or edited the main substance of the Anglican prayer book, saw deeper than this. They realised that the real asceticism is an asceticism of the spirit, meaningless without the co-operation of the human will. Yet, like the 'Orphics', they could not wipe out all the past. They must still retain the 'laudable custom' of fasting communion and vegetarian Lent as concessions to the conservative spirit in human nature. The ecclesiastical golden age is always in antiquity.

γ. *Moral eschatology and cosmology.* The third corollary of Personal Sin is the need for a moral explanation of the universe and a moral theory of its origin. A sinless religion like that of Homer is always anthropocentric: the macrocosm presents no problems because it is regarded merely as a scenic setting for the microcosm. Whence came the world and man? Whither do they go? are questions Achilles and Odysseus never dreamed of asking. But no sooner does a concept of sin enter the human mind than simultaneously there arises the need, on the one hand of an eschatology, on the other of a cosmogony. In

[1] St Gregory, *Dial.* I, 10 (see also Muratori, *Antich. Ital. Diss.* xx).

'Orphism' the numerous descents into Hades, one of which has actually been interpolated into the *Odyssey*,[1] testify to the former; while the myths of the Titans and the World-Egg bear witness of the latter need. Nearly all religions, in which a sense of sin is fundamental, conceive of the after-life as a lurid process of purification by ordeal—purgatory for all, Hell fire for many, eternal bliss for the chosen few. In sinless religions the existence after death is a vague and dreamy state in which Being and Not-Being are almost merged in one. "I know", says Achilles of the ghost of Patroclus, "that the soul exists after physical death; but it is only an image, bereft of feeling and intelligence."[2] In any case, all perils can be charmed away by holocausts and libations. One hesitates here to draw the parallel between old and new. Can one fairly claim that mediaeval Catholicism was a sinless religion, and that Protestantism, introducing sin for the first time, brought in its train a more hideous eschatology? I fear not. The Hell fire which threatened the monk in his cell was no less horrible than that which tormented the conscience of the Puritan in his study. The most to be said is this: perhaps

[1] *Od.* XI, 565–627 (said to be interpolated by Onomacritus).

[2] *Iliad*, XXIII, 103:

ὦ πόποι ἦ ῥά τις ἔστι καὶ εἰν Ἀΐδαο δόμοισι
ψυχὴ καὶ εἴδωλον, ἀτὰρ φρένες οὐκ ἔνι πάμπαν.

the Catholic had more faith in the apotropaic powers of his sacraments than the Protestant had in his own 'will to be good'. Certainly a Grand Inquisitor would have experienced difficulty in rivalling the Calvinistic Hell.

The parallel at the other extreme of human life is between 'Orphic' cosmogony and the Garden of Eden. There had been no cosmogony in Homer, at any rate in the *Iliad* and *Odyssey*—but the 'Orphics' introduced a complicated myth, by which Ἔρως, 'the Spirit of God moving over the waters', created the world; while the Dionysiac and Titanic elements accounted for good and evil. The most commonly accepted story is this: first came Time, from whom sprang Ether and Chaos. Out of Ether and Chaos, Time formed a silver egg. Out of the egg sprang Ἔρως, or in other versions, Phanes, god of light. The development of the world was a self-revelation of this power. Phanes was next swallowed by Zeus. The latter by Persephone had a son Dionysus. Dionysus was pursued by Titans and took the form of a bull, which the Titans rent to pieces. Athene saved the bull's heart, which Zeus swallowed in order to beget a new Dionysus. The Titans, stained by the blood of the bull Dionysus, were struck down by the lightning flash of Zeus; and out of their ashes sprang the race of men—which thereby contained both the Titanic element (the spirit of evil) and the Dionysiac (the spirit of good).[1] This myth found its way into the ἱεροὶ λόγοι, the 'Orphic' Bible, and was regarded with the same veneration as the Adam-Eve legend in Genesis. It appears too, by inference, on the golden tablets of lower Italy; in such verses as "I am a child of earth and starry heaven, but my race is of heaven alone".[2] Euripides preserves the essentials of the same cosmogony in a fragment of Melanippe the Wise.[3] Man is a fallen creature by reason of his association with the earthly and phenomenal, but he contains the spark of divine fire within him; and the ultimate home from whence he came, and whither he will return, is Heaven it-self.

The relation between Homer and 'Orphism' is repeated in a different setting, and with many variations because history never repeats itself mechanically, in the parallelism between Catholic and Protestant. The mediaeval Church believed in the fall of man, and accepted theoretically the aetiological myth of Adam and Eve; but these

[1] It will be at once obvious that this myth is purely aetiological—a very clumsy attempt to harmonise the 'Orphic' Ἔρως with the Olympian Zeus on one hand, and with Dionysus on the other.

[2] Petelia tablet (No. 1):

γῆς πάϊς εἰμὶ καὶ οὐρανοῦ ἀστερόεντος
αὐτὰρ ἐμοὶ γένος οὐράνιον.

[3] Eur. fr. 484 (Nauck):

κοὐκ ἐμὸς ὁ μῦθος, ἀλλ' ἐμῆς μητρὸς πάρα κ.τ.λ.

doctrines never assumed the pre-eminent importance which they acquired in Protestant Christianity, if only because the Bible in the Middle
Ages was almost completely superseded by the
dogmas of the hierarchy. Prelates and ecclesiastics were naturally concerned to emphasise the
sacramental and priestly side of theology. It was
not until the Reformation that stress was laid
on the more personal and individualistic philosophy of Fallen Man.

(3) REVERENCE FOR SACRED SCRIPTURES

The reference to the Garden of Eden and a
legend of cosmogony suggests the more extensive
problem of sacred writings in general. That
'Orphism' was essentially and fundamentally a
'book religion' is indicated by many testimonies.
In the play of Euripides, Theseus, upbraiding
Hippolytus for his ascetic principles, says "Take
Orpheus as thy king, play the Bacchanal, and
worship the thin smoke of *many scriptures*".[1] In
the second book of the *Republic*, Adimantus tells
of the itinerant mystery-mongers who "produce
a whole host of *books* by Musaeus and Orpheus—
the offspring as they say of the Moon and the
Muses—using these as the authority for their

---

[1] Eur. *Hipp.* 953:

$$\text{'Ορφέα τ' ἄνακτ' ἔχων}$$
$$\text{βάκχευε πολλῶν γραμμάτων τιμῶν καπνούς.}$$

ritual".[1] Plutarch, in describing a dinner-table conversation as to which came first, the hen or the egg, puts these words into the mouth of Alexander the Epicurean: "I shall sing to those who know the sacred Orphic *scripture*, which affirms that the egg only is older than the bird".[2] This last testimony suggests in greater detail the nature of the 'Orphic' scriptures—they have something to do with a World-Egg, a theory of creation. The evidence supplied by Proclus' commentary on Plato's *Timaeus* confirms such a view.[3] The Neoplatonists appear to have known of a 'Rhapsodic Theogony', based on the earlier ἱεροὶ λόγοι, which sets forth in detail the whole scriptural foundation of the 'Orphic' religion—the myth of the World-Egg, explaining the origin of cosmic order; the successions of the gods; and the legend of the divine son Dionysus-Zagreus.

On the score of sacred writings, therefore, the parallel between ancient and modern seems complete. In the ancient world we have the religion of Homer, entirely concerned with sacrifice and ritual, entirely dominated by the note of 'Confiteor'—the confession of vows duly performed: and over against it the religion of 'Orpheus',

[1] *Rep.* 364e: βίβλων δὲ ὅμαδον παρέχονται Μουσαίου καὶ Ὀρφέως...καθ᾽ ἃς θυηπολοῦσι.

[2] Plutarch, *Symposiacs*, II, 3, 1: τὸν Ὀρφικὸν καὶ ἱερὸν λόγον, ὃς ἐξ ὄρνιθος μόνον τὸ ὠὸν ἀποφαίνει πρεσβύτερον.

[3] Proclus, *in Tim.* II, 307 *sq.*

which emphasised the relation of the individual soul with God, for authority turning not to priests but scriptures. In the more modern world we have the mediaeval Church, a picturesque and colourful religious system based on sacerdotalism and ecclesiolatry: over against it the Protestant reformers with their 'justification by faith' and bibliolatrous attitude to the canonical writings. An objection may be raised that Homer, surely, not 'Orpheus', was the Bible of the Greeks. For civil and literary purposes, yes; for religious purposes, no. The fourth century orator Lycurgus, in his speech against Leocrates, tells us that Homer was recited regularly at the Panathenaia;[1] much in the same way as passages from the Bible are declaimed when a school, a college or a city commemorates its benefactors. We read too in Xenophon of the perfectly educated young Greek who knew Homer by heart,[2] just as Oxford and Cambridge undergraduates of the nineteenth century knew the Psalms. Homer moulded Greek literary tradition, no less than the poetical books of the Authorised Version have moulded our own; but only the superficial thinker would attach to this any religious significance. Homer offered no comfort for the soul: he did not even present a philosophy of creation and human life.

[1] Lycurgus, *in Leocratem*, 102.
[2] Xenophon, *Symposium*.

For that we must turn to the ἱεροὶ λόγοι of the 'Orphics'.

(4) LOCALISED RELIGION

A further parallelism between the 'Orphic' and the Protestant as against the Homeric and the Catholic is *à propos* of localised religion and national churches. That the mediaeval Church and the Olympic pantheon were in respect of place widespread—almost universal—in their influence, needs little proving. The Bishop of Rome held sway over the whole of Western Europe: Zeus, Poseidon, Apollo, Artemis and their company were worshipped, with the same significance if under different names, in Asia Minor and Thrace no less than in Boeotia and the Peloponnese. Protestantism on the other hand was not universal. It flourished in Great Britain, France, Holland, Belgium, Germany, Switzerland; but in each case it acquired a peculiarly local colour. The Calvinism taught in Geneva was not merely specifically different from the Lutheranism in Germany. It was almost a genus of its own. How far is this true of 'Orphism'? Prof. Cornford writes:[1] "Orphism was a free religion. Not only was it, like the Eleusinian mysteries, independent of the social structure of the civic community, but, unlike those mysteries,

[1] *Camb. Anc. Hist.* IV, 532.

it was not localized at any sanctuary. In consequence of this detachment, it could spread wherever the theological literature which it produced in considerable volume found willing readers". That it was "a free religion", we have already seen from its dissenting nature; but that it was "not localized at any sanctuary" needs further investigation. It will be proved by the evidence, I think, that 'Orphism' *was* localised. As a general phenomenon, not necessarily connected with a historical 'Orpheus', it was found mainly in these centres: Thrace, Lesbos, Athens, Eleusis, Lerna, Phlya, South Italy and Sicily, and Crete. We hear very little of 'Orphic' influence at Delphi. At Sparta too it seems to have been unknown. Herodotus tells of Demaratus and the Lacedaemonian army marching through the Thriasian plain when the mystic cry of Iacchus was heard from Eleusis. The king asked what the noise might be, "not being conversant with the rites of Eleusis".[1]

Moreover, just as the Calvinists were different from the Lutherans, and the Lutherans again from the Huguenots; so the 'Orphism' at Lesbos was different from that at Eleusis, and that at Eleusis from that in South Italy. It was not, like

[1] Her. VIII, 65: εἶναι δ' ἀδαήμονα τῶν ἱρῶν τῶν ἐν Ἐλευσῖνι γινομένων τὸν Δημάρητον, εἰρέσθαι τε αὐτὸν ὅ τι τὸ φθεγγόμενον εἴη τοῦτο.

Catholicism, a uniform creed, independent of its setting. At Lesbos, emphasis was laid on the hero shrine and the oracular cult of the singing head, 'Orpheus' being regarded primarily as a μάντις. At Eleusis, the dominant note was sacramental: 'Orphism' became almost synonymous with mystic initiation or communion, and great prominence was attached to a sublimated form of sexual symbolism called the Sacred Marriage. In Italy, to judge from our evidence, the religion of 'Orpheus' was specially characterised by its pietistic and eschatological notes. The rule of the saints at Croton testifies to the rigid cult of ὁσιότης, while the golden tablets bear witness to the intense yearning for the after life. At Athens, where society fell into two main classes, οἱ φιλόσοφοι and οἱ πολλοί, 'Orphism' took the form either of a vague, ascetic and mystical monotheism on the one hand; or a degraded, quasi-magical charlatanry on the other. In Thrace, the wild, elemental and naturalistic spirit was uppermost: at Phlya the worship of Ἔρως predominates—'the spirit of God moving over the waters'. Though 'Orphism' may have been independent of the political structure, it was clearly not independent of the sociological background of the civic communities.

(5) A MORE SPIRITUAL CONCEPTION OF COMMUNION

The mention made above of mystic communions and sacred marriages at Eleusis suggests two further parallels between the old and the new. Let us examine first the idea of communion. The original sacramental meal of the religion of Dionysus was both savage and superstitious; it was an ὠμοφαγία, a devouring of raw bull's flesh. The details of this hideous ceremony have been preserved by so many and independent authorities that its historicity is established beyond every shadow of doubt. Clement of Alexandria was no doubt biassed and excessively vehement in his denunciations of paganism, but if the rhetoric is purged away, certain trustworthy facts remain. "The Bacchanals", he says,[1] "have orgiastic rites in worship of Dionysus the Mad: they celebrate the holy days of the month with a feast of raw flesh; which rite is performed by the distribution of the butchered animal, the votaries being crowned with serpents and shrieking out the mystic cry 'Eua'." Euripides too makes his chorus in the *Cretans* sing of "the joy of the bull-god slain".[2] That such sacramental meals were

[1] *Exhortation*, II, 12: ὀργιάζουσι...ὠμοφαγίᾳ τὴν ἱερομηνίαν ἄγοντες.

[2] *Cretans*, fr. 203 (apud Porphyry, *de abst.* IV, 19):
καὶ νυκτιπόλου Ζαγρέως βροντὰς
τάς τ' ὠμοφάγους δαῖτας τελέσας.

held in Thrace and Crete, we know for certain:
it is exceedingly probable that they were cele-
brated at Eleusis too, before the refining influence of 'Orphism' was felt. Plato in the
Critias[1] describes a ritual of bull sacrifice and
sacrament which scholars think took place at
Eleusis;[2] the evidence of an Attic inscription confirms such a view;[3] and Cratinus, an Athenian
initiate, is called by Aristophanes 'bull-eater'.[4]

About the sixth century a movement of reform
seems to have begun. How far it was the effect
of agriculture, how far it was due to the influence
of Demeter, how far to the advent of 'Orphism'
is hard to say. That 'Orphism' did come into
being at Eleusis, either spontaneously or from
without, is demonstrable from the peculiarly
'Orphic' ceremonies of the λικνοφορία and ἱερὸς
γάμος. That the sacrament became no longer a
blood feast but more and more a vegetarian meal
is seen from the evidence of a Homeric hymn,
where the Earth Mother, refusing even rich red
wine, drinks only water mixed with meal.[5] As

[1] *Critias*, 119e *sq.*

[2] See von Fritze in *Beiträge*, pp. 514, 563; also J. E.
Harrison, *Prolegomena*, p. 546.

[3] *C.I.A.* II, 467: ἤραντο δὲ τοῖς Μυστηρίοις τοὺς βοῦς ἐν
Ἐλευσῖνι τῇ θυσίᾳ.

[4] *Frogs*, 355: μηδὲ Κρατίνου τοῦ ταυροφάγου γλώττης βακ-
χεῖ' ἐτελέσθη.

[5] *Hymn to Demeter*, 207: ἄνωγε δ' ἄρ' ἄλφι καὶ ὕδωρ
δοῦναι μίξασαν πιέμεν γλήχωνι τερείνῃ.

time goes on, the communion idea at Eleusis becomes by degrees purged of its old crudity and barbarous savagery.[1] It still remains to a certain degree superstitious; but the superstition is more refined, more spiritual, more sublimated. The threefold commandment comes to the fore which later tradition assigned to Triptolemus. "Honour your parents, worship the gods with *fruits, do not injure animals.*" I can only suggest that the change is due to 'Orphism'.

The modern counterpart is seen in the gradual evolution of Eucharistic doctrine between the fourteenth and seventeenth centuries in the Protestant countries of Western Europe. There was never of course any approach to rites so savage as the Thracian and Cretan ὠμοφαγίαι; but Protestantism brought the same sublimating influence into Catholicism as 'Orphism' brought into the religion of Dionysus. Eucharistic vestments and ritual suggestive of the old sacramental theory tended to disappear: rubrics were introduced which breathed the spirit of *Panis es et panis manebis*: emphasis was laid more and more

[1] Chief authorities are the schol. on *Gorgias*, 407 c; Clem. Alex. *Exhortation*, p. 18 (reading ἐγγευσάμενος); and a vase at Naples reproduced by Farnell, *Cults*, III, Plate 15 b. Scholars disagree as to whether there was any communion with the divine implied. Jevons and Jane Harrison say there was; H. J. Rose thinks not. Possibly the initiates differed in their attitude to the ceremony, as High and Low Anglicans differ to-day.

on the *subjective* state of the recipient, and the *heavenly* meaning of the outward symbols. The last vestiges of the mediaeval Mass remained in such prayers as that "we may evermore dwell in Him and He in us"—and even these have become refined and spiritualised by time and association.

(6) SUBLIMATED SEX-WORSHIP

The second parallel suggested by a glance at the 'Orphic' ceremonial at Eleusis is concerned with the Sacred Marriage. Here, we enter for the most part the realm of speculation; owing to the secrecy which surrounded this rite, and the consequent lack of first-hand, unbiassed, and strictly scientific information. Such conclusions as can be reached will have as their basis the somewhat enigmatic utterances of ancient writers, interpreted by ourselves in the light of comparison with similar religions of which our knowledge is happily more extensive. The fundamental fact that *some sort of* sacred marriage was enacted, at dead of night, in the initiation chamber at Eleusis, is established by several testimonies.[1] As an example we will record that of Asterius (fourth century A.D.), who writes: "Is there not a descent into the darkness, and the sacred and

[1] For sources see Lobeck, *Aglaophamus* (1829) and M. P. Foucart, *Les grands mystères d'Eleusis* (1900).

solitary intercourse of hierophant and priestess?"[1]
It is on the problem of interpretation that scholars
differ. The most likely explanation, supported by
the recent sociological researches of Freud and
his school, seems to be this. All men, primitive
men especially, tend to make God in their own
image. Accordingly, if their own life is organised
on a family basis by which father co-operates
with mother to bring forth a new human being,
this sexual principle will be reflected in their
religion. The need of such expression is demonstrable at all stages of social and intellectual
development. Very primitive peoples, typified by
certain castes of Ceylonese at the present day,
are content with an open and undisguised worship of the generative organs of man. As civilisation advances, frankness of this kind comes to
be regarded with suspicion, and a cloak of respectability is thrown over everything in the form
of secret societies, entrance to which can only
be gained by initiation.[2] Such secret societies in
the ancient world are the 'Orphic' θίασοι. Finally

---

[1] Asterius, *Encom. Martyr.* 113 b: οὐκ ἐκεῖ καταβάσιον τὸ
σκοτεινὸν καὶ αἱ σεμναὶ τοῦ ἱεροφάντου πρὸς τὴν ἱερείαν συντυχίαι
μόνου πρὸς μόνην; This evidence *may* be discounted, on the
grounds of lateness.

[2] This is, I think, a more likely origin of secret societies
than that suggested by Kern (*Die Religion der Griechen*, I,
1926). Kern thinks that the Hellenic invaders inflicted
persecution on the early Greek religion and drove its
votaries to secrecy.

the whole idea becomes mysticised and spiritualised, until what was originally an object of superstitious reverence becomes nothing more than
the symbol of an abstract power in nature. At
Eleusis there was a *substratum* of the primitive
and elemental.[1] Pausanias, more sensitive because he lived in a more civilised age, shrinks
from an explanation. After describing the cult of
the Bean-man, he remarks, "Whosoever has seen
the rite at Eleusis or read the so-called 'Writings
of Orpheus' knows what I mean".[2] But over and
above the primitive *substratnm* there was a more
spiritual idea for which 'Orphism' was probably
responsible. The ceremonial became more and
more a mimetic representation of the myths of
Mother and Son—Semele and Dionysus, Brimo
and Brimos—the beautiful symbolism of Ἔρως at
work in human creation. "Lady Brimo hath
born a sacred son Brimos",[3] cried the celebrant,
and in the worship of speechless contemplation
the initiate became at one with primordial love.[4]

---

[1] H. J. Rose is inclined to reject the whole idea of sexual
symbolism in the Sacred Marriage on the grounds of
unreliable evidence (see article on 'Mysteries' in *Encyc.
Brit.*). Jane Harrison establishes its historicity to my mind
beyond all shadow of doubt (*Prolegomena*, pp. 535 *sq.*).

[2] Paus. I, 37, 4: ὅστις δὲ ἤδη τελετὴν Ἐλευσῖνι εἶδεν ἢ τὰ
καλούμενα Ὀρφικὰ ἐπελέξατο, οἶδεν ὃ λέγω.

[3] Pseudo-Hippolytus, *Philosophoumena*, v, 8: ἱερὸν ἔτεκε
πότνια κοῦρον Βριμὼ Βριμόν. This may be Gnostic.

[4] That an *emotional* experience took place is clear from
the language of Aristotle, fr. 45: παθεῖν καὶ διατεθῆναι.

In the minds of philosophers pregnant with the 'Orphic' spirit, a far loftier height was reached—nothing less than the ἱερὸς γάμος of the soul with God. Read the myth of Diotima in Plato's *Symposium*; an allegory of the Eleusinian rites,[1] where the vision is laid up in Heaven itself—an ideal beauty, pure, unmixed, not infected by the colour of humanity.

The need for ceremonial expression of the sexual principle in human nature is not confined to antiquity. It is still flourishing. There are secret societies to-day which cater for the same impulses as Eleusis did in the past. A modernised form of sex worship, stripped of superstition and religious significance, but nevertheless retaining all the old crudity and repulsiveness, survives in those initiation ceremonies which penetrate much deeper than mere tar and feathers.[2] I do not know whether there is a sexual element in Masonry, but at least in other respects there is a striking similarity between an 'Orphic' θίασος and a Masonic lodge. The parallel in Christianity, as we might hope, is more refined. There is no trace of open sex worship, but there are visible signs of

---

[1] Note such phrases as in 210a: ταῦτα μὲν οὖν τὰ ἐρωτικὰ ἴσως, ὦ Σώκρατες, κἂν σὺ μυηθείης· τὰ δὲ τέλεα καὶ ἐποπτικά... οὐκ οἶδ' εἰ οἷός τ' ἂν εἴης.

[2] Initiation ceremonies of this kind are common, I am told, in some of the modern universities, and in badly disciplined theological colleges.

sexual imagery—dim reflections of paganism—more elemental and primary in Catholicism, more mystical and spiritualised in Protestantism. The Catholic Trinity was in the Middle Ages not God, Jesus Christ and the Holy Ghost, but God, Jesus Christ and the Virgin Mary—Father, Son and Mother. Great stress, almost amounting to a religion in itself, was laid on such doctrines as the Immaculate Conception and the Virgin Birth. The sexual note was sounded also in the monk or nun being 'wedded to the Church'. Protestantism retained much of this, but it was theoretically so neglected that in practice it almost disappeared. The Virginity of Mary is seldom mentioned in Protestant churches, except in the Anglican creeds and the liturgies for her holy days. A sexual image still retained is the beautiful metaphor of St Paul: the Church as the bride of Christ.

(7) EMPHASIS ON HUMANITARIAN VALUES

The last parallel that I would draw between the ancient 'Orphic' and the modern Protestant is their essential humanitarianism. I do not suggest that the divine or metaphysical play *no* part in their respective philosophical systems: on the contrary we have already examined such ultra-mundane aspects of their belief as the concept of Hell and divine judgment. Neither am I concerned to dispute with Maass and Jane Harrison whether 'Orpheus' was god or man: that is a problem which, with our present supply of evidence, can scarcely be solved. I would merely point out that, all things considered, the ancient 'Orphic' and the modern Protestant *tend* to emphasise the human, the personal, the subjective, rather than the divine, the supernatural and the miraculous. The 'grace' which religion offers can be of various types—it can be active, it can be passive, or it can be a mixture of both active and passive. Can a man become acceptable to God by holy living and nothing more? If so, he is a recipient of 'active' grace. Can he achieve the same end by means of supernatural, miraculous gifts bestowed by a priesthood? If so, he receives 'passive' grace. Must he combine both personal piety and sacerdotal blessing? If so, neither 'active' nor 'passive' grace are by themselves enough. The traditional religion of Dionysus, and its more civilised counterpart, the mediaeval Church, laid supreme stress on 'passive' grace. The possibility of an individual finding his way to the divine by the light of conscience alone was foreign to their way of thought. The human conscience as the criterion of human action barely existed. If it did exist, it was always subordinate to the supernatural guidance of ritual and priesthood.

The religion of 'Orpheus' and the Protestant reformers brought a change. It cannot truly be said that they abolished 'passive' grace and took their stand on 'active' grace alone, because a certain element of the priestly and ritualistic was still retained.[1] It is, however, demonstrable from our evidence that the 'active' became more and more; the 'passive' less and less, important. When Pythagoras (who on the ethical side was clearly influenced by 'Orphism') examined his own soul, he did not make a confession of ritual acts duly performed—as for instance the mystic at Eleusis did.[2] He asked himself "what he had done amiss, and what aright; what had he omitted that he ought to have performed".[3] He examined his *conscience*; his *will*; his personal, subjective, capacity to work good or evil. Aristophanes in his dramatic scenes is usually an unreliable authority, but in his choruses, where the satirical tone yields place to the more sober and gentler lyric, his testimony is perhaps worthy of consideration. In the *Frogs* the chorus sing "On us alone the sun and gracious daylight shine, who are initiated and live a holy life".[4] Salvation requires not

[1] E.g. the necessity of baptism and initiation for salvation.
[2] See schol. on Plato, *Gorgias*, 407c; Clem. Alex. *Exhortation*, 18.
[3] D. Laert. *Pythagoras*, 22: πῇ παρέβην; τί δ' ἔρεξα; τί μοι δέον οὐκ ἐτελέσθη;
[4] *Frogs*, 455: ὅσοι μεμυήμεθ' εὐσεβῆ τε διάγομεν τρόπον.

initiation alone, but a holy life also—an εὐσεβὴς τρόπος, 'a way of life marked by fair reverence'; not an ἁγνὸς τρόπος, 'a way of life ritually clean', nor again an ὅσιος τρόπος, 'a consecrated way of life'. Again, take the evidence of Andocides in his speech on the Mysteries. "You have been initiated", he says, "and you have seen the 'sacra' of the two deities, *in order that you may punish the impious, and preserve such as commit no injustice*".[1] A mere rhetorical appeal in the interests of the case? If this passage was unique, perhaps such an explanation might be accepted. But further on we read of a lady whom the divinities at Eleusis had made so upright and morally good that she "thought it behoved her to die rather than look on the shameless conduct of a man".[2] The sophist Libanius also tells us that the initiates must be "pure of soul".[3]

CONCLUSION

It would be rash to maintain that 'Orphism' ever achieved such a high ideal of personal holiness as that of Socrates or Epictetus. It was bound from the nature of things to remain pri-

---

[1] *De mysteriis*, 31: μεμύησθε...ἵνα τιμωρήσητε μὲν τοὺς ἀσεβοῦντας, σώζητε δὲ τοὺς μηδὲν ἀδικοῦντας.

[2] *Ibid.* 125: καὶ οὗτος μὲν...οὐκ ἔδεισε τὼ θεώ· ἡ δὲ τοῦ Ἰσχομάχου θυγάτηρ τεθνάναι νομίσασα λυσιτελεῖν ἢ ζῆν ὁρῶσα τὰ γινόμενα.

[3] Libanius, IV, 356.

mitive, and even barbarous, in certain aspects. It never completely severed its association with Dionysus, any more than Protestantism has ever severed its association with the Catholic element in tradition. It never quite rid itself of the degrading, the priggish, and the superstitious; but as long as human nature remains imperfect, what faith ever will? On the other hand, as a movement of reform and an attempt to establish the relation of the individual soul with God as the only real basis of religion and morality, it is a noble phenomenon in ancient history and worthy of deeper study.

EPILOGUE

'ORPHISM' AND THE PRESENT DAY

'ORPHISM' AND THE PRESENT DAY

The question has been, and still is, often asked:
"What profit is there in a religion dead and gone?
What relation can it conceivably bear to the
ever-changing stream of modern thought? Has it
any reality except for the pedant and the scholar?
Can it be said to represent even the ancient Greek
mind at its best?" It might be well, therefore,
before we close, to sit as it were with half-closed
eyes, and contemplate 'Orphism' as an idea in
all time: straining to free it, as far as may be,
from the fetters which bind it to a particular
place at a particular moment in antiquity; trying
to raise it out of the realm of the merely historical
to the higher realm of thought and poetry.

First let us rescue it from the shadows of
obscurity in its own age and civilisation. It has
been traditional in the past to regard everything
Greek as necessarily and essentially Apolline.
The Agias of Lysippus and the Olympians of
Pindar have been taken to represent the ideal
type of Hellenic art and thought from Homer to
Theophrastus; while Plato, because of his affini-
ties with mysticism and Pauline Christianity, has
been called "the most un-Greek of all the Greeks".
This method of generalisation, I maintain, has
led to a one-sided and distorted view of the

ancient intellect, and to a narrowing of its catholicity of outlook. The ancient Greek could be, and often was, as mystically minded as the Neoplatonists at Alexandria or the Monastics at Siena. 'Orpheus', Pythagoras, Plato, Philo and Plotinus may almost be taken to represent a continuous tradition of mysticism, which was never without its followers among the philosophic, or its admirers among the multitude. It may be urged, with some degree of truth, that such mysticism was from the start a foreign and Oriental importation; but in the course of time it became so assimilated by genuinely Hellenic thought that Plato inherited it as an inseparable characteristic of his country's philosophic and literary tradition.

But to go further than this, what relation has 'Orphism' to the present day? Should we of the twentieth century be happier or better for being more 'Orphic'? Yes and no. To revive the *minutiae* of 'Orphic' ceremonial, to daub ourselves with clay, and to preach that the body is a tomb, would be a step towards degradation. On the other hand, to imitate the best and purest elements in this all-embracing philosophy would be, I think, a positive gain. 'Orphism', because it was a religion of revolt, discarded all traditional forms *quâ* traditional forms and showed that, in the mind of a free and spiritually minded man, they can have no real meaning. They are only so much clap-trap—the ready tool of greedy ecclesiastics and unscrupulous politicians. The genuine philosopher transcends these, as the Idea of the Good in Plato transcends the Ideas of Mud and Dirt. If the modern mind could recapture the 'Orphic' spirit in this respect, and apply it to such institutions as Marriage and Divorce, Capital and Labour, Teacher and Taught, Parent and Child, Clergy and Laity, Professional and Artisan, Patrician and Plebeian, Legitimate and Illegitimate, it would be freed from many bogeys and evil spirits which thwart its happiness and disturb its peaceful state of ἀταραξία.

Viewed as an abstract idea, 'Orphism' strikes three major notes on the scale of our appreciative sense—the note of mysticism, the note of light, and the note of tranquillity. All these are of immense value for the present day.

The note of mysticism carries with it not the slightest hint of obscurantism, still less of theurgy. It is concerned with the feeling for spiritual values, the Good, the True and the Beautiful, especially the Good and the Beautiful. It awakens a response similar to that provoked by the Enneads of Plotinus; and, on the whole, it is inseparable from the cult of abstinence and the ascetic life. I do not suggest that modern civilisation would be necessarily improved by the

77

imposition of a taboo on beans, still less by the superstitious avoidance of birth and death. At the same time I think that there is something quaintly beautiful about the 'Orphic' reverence for animals, and something picturesque about their mystic cult of ὁσιότης. The twentieth century has still much to learn concerning the sanctity of animate life; and, although mechanically its aeroplanes have penetrated to the farthest heights of celestial aether, intellectually it still remains on the comparatively low level of grammatical terms and logical concepts. The dizzier heights of spiritual ideas have yet to be explored. Let us learn a lesson from the noble image of the 'Orphic' Ἔρως, Platonised and idealised in the *Symposium*: "Nor again will our initiate find the beautiful presented to him in the guise of a face or of hands or any other portion of the body, nor as a particular description or piece of knowledge, nor as existing somewhere in another substance, such as an animal or the earth or sky or any other thing; but existing ever in singularity of form, independent by itself, while all the multitude of beautiful things partake of it in such wise that, though all of them are coming to be and perishing, it grows neither greater nor less, and is affected by nothing".[1]

[1] Plato, *Symposium*, 211a (Loeb translation): οὐδ' αὖ φαντασθήσεται....

Second, the note of light. 'Orpheus' is represented in later mythology as descending to the murky depths of the underworld to recover Eurydice; but that is not the real 'Orpheus'. The real 'Orpheus' is the minstrel of vase paintings, who sits with lyre in hand and contemplates the sun. 'Orphism' is a religion of light—not the gay and jovial light of the Anthesteria or Thargelia, which go no further than colourful ritual and pageantry, concealing all the while deep-rooted springs of fear and superstition; but a purer, more unadulterated light whose source is ὁσιότης and ὁμοίωσις τῷ θεῷ. Whoever has watched a procession of Corpus Christi pass through the streets of Rome or Florence, must feel that Latin Europe still has much to learn from 'Orpheus'. Modern Italy reproduces the Anthesteria in all its resplendent imagery. There are flowers and sweet perfumes, statues of a goddess crowned with garlands, public holiday—in fact all the outward appearances of joy and brightness. But the light is only colourful darkness.

Third, the note of tranquillity. Critics have frequently commended the serene dignity of the Parthenon Theseus, and the unruffled calm of the Hermes of Praxiteles, as typical of the Greek genius at its best. Yet these are not 'Orphic', neither is their peace of mind worthy of imitation; for beneath the surface they reflect the sensuousness of a civilisation which had little or no respect for women, and which escaped the roughening influence of manual labour by the universal institution of slavery. There is nothing sensuous or morally relaxing about the tranquillity of 'Orpheus'. Kingsley is reproducing the wrong spirit when he tells how, beneath the spell of the minstrel god, the heroes "closed their heavy eyes; and dreamed of bright, still gardens, and of slumbers under murmuring pines, till all their toil seemed foolishness, and they thought of their renown no more".[1] Kingsley has romanticised 'Orpheus', just as Keats romanticised the Grecian urn. There is nothing romantic about the real 'Orpheus'. His tranquillity is, above all, restrained and sober. It is a state of peace which flows naturally from the life of self-discipline and communion with the source of infinite Ἔρως, losing its coldness in brotherly affection, and its austerity in tenderness to brute creation. Bacon is nearer to the truth when he says that the tale of 'Orpheus' "may seem to represent the image of philosophy".[2]

[1] Kingsley, *Argonauts*, Part 5.
[2] Bacon, *Wisdom of the Ancients*, XI.

www.ingramcontent.com/pod-product-compliance
Ingram Content Group UK Ltd.
Pitfield, Milton Keynes, MK11 3LW, UK
UKHW020447010325
455719UK00015B/466